When in the
Course of
Human Events

Malcolm Boyd

and twice Pulitzer Prize-winner

Paul Conrad

When in the Course of Human Events

SHEED AND WARD, INC.

Subsidiary of Universal Press Syndicate

Copyright 1973
Sheed and Ward, Inc.
Subsidiary of Universal Press Syndicate
475 Fifth Avenue, New York 10017

ISBN: 0-8362-0558-8

Library of Congress Card Number 73-11507
Printed in the United States of America
by NAPCO Graphic Arts, Inc.

To Kay

Introduction

Paul Conrad has stood for more than two decades in a conspicuous and vulnerable position at the complex junction of journalism and the American public. His classic portraits of people and social situations are profoundly prophetic ones, combining fearless criticism with compassion.

Because they superbly depict universal truths delineated in highly specific symbols, these cartoon-portraits address a vast public. I suppose that many thousands of his men and women readers struggle to discern meanings in life and make responsible decisions.

Ignazio Silone has remarked poignantly: "In the sacred history of man on earth, it is still, alas, Good Friday." A sober humanist, Jew or Christian, must confront his or her own conscience as well as the demands of society in the process of decision-making, private and public. Albert Camus spoke to this need when he wrote: "I should like to be able to love my country and still love justice." Criticism of the state can be a high form of honoring it. Indeed, to turn one's back on the problems and tragedies of society is to dishonor the state. Moral renewal can come only from within the deliberately shared experience—the vision, pain, joy and hope—of scarred and struggling people.

Paul Conrad has long understood the connections between prayers and life, the sacred and the secular, human ideals and actions. Our collaboration in these pages is a celebration of friendship and a testament of our hope.

Malcolm Boyd

When in the
Course of
Human Events

Save us from the web of conspiracy that chokes truth, Lord.

Save us from the web of power that chokes honor.

Save us from the web of self-delusion that chokes awareness of right and wrong.

Save us from the lie whose threads are as strong as steel, Lord.

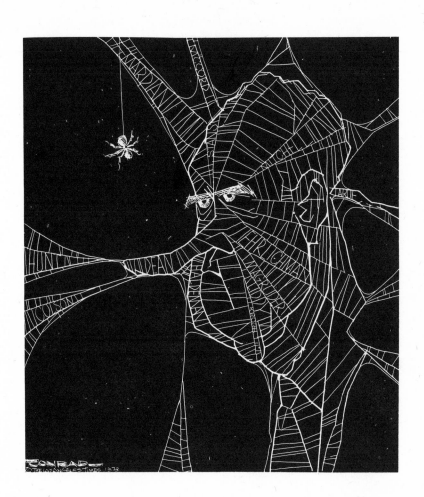

Help me not to be dead while I am still
alive, Lord.

"What did you do to stop the war, daddy?"

Your geniuses amaze me, Lord, and evoke both my fervent admiration and then dismaying envy.

Evil geniuses terrify me when I contemplate the horror they are capable of bringing to the world.

Geniuses who create beauty, stretch our minds, refocus our visions, and speak to us about peace, seem to be among your saints, Christ.

Oh, freedom

Lord! Don't let us lose it.
Lord! Don't let us give it away.
Lord! Make us struggle for it.

" . . . Copy Boy. . . . !"

" . . . Son . . . !"   " . . . Dad . . . !"

Dad is a phony, Jesus.

Why do some of us have to be phony humans, Lord, and mistreat ourselves as if we were engines?

But we're not, Christ. We're people. Can we learn how to treat ourselves that way?

"Whoever receives one such child in my name receives me."
    Jesus, help us to receive you.

Nothing unusual happened on the way to school again
today . . .

I don't understand how people can talk about love without justice, Lord.
   Do you?

"When . . . in . . . the . . . course . . . of . . . human . . . events."

You lost in Vietnam, didn't you, Christ?
Why do we say that we won?

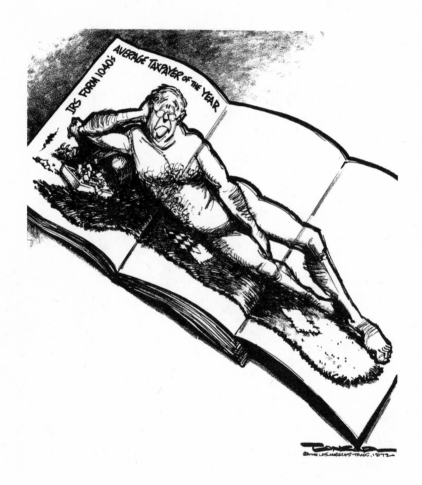

We are all so naked and vulnerable, amusing and tragic, aren't we, Lord?

Anything that enhances our dignity as your creation, or preserves our rights as persons, is deeply appreciated.

" . . . Four more weeks! . . . Four more weeks! . . . "

Why don't we ever learn, Lord, that you
hear everything in the heavens and in the earth?

Can we creatively use technology, Lord, instead of let it uncreatively misuse us?

Shake us, Jesus! Awaken us to the challenge and excitement of living.

Enable us to see complex people instead of simple images, Christ.

Enable us to be complex people instead of simple images, Christ.

You know nothing about Watergate, which group would you most likely suspect of burglary, theft, breaking and entering, wiretapping, election law violations and conspiracy?

Thanks for reminding us, Jesus, that love and justice, rights and equal opportunity, are meant to be spread around.

Why do people want to construct cages
for ideas, Lord?

Ideas need freedom to roam around at will.
Ideas need fresh air and sunlight. Ideas need
exercise and nourishment.

Christ, I want to smash these bars.

Where there is liberty, Lord, it is your gift.
Where there is justice, Lord, it is your gift.
Teach us not to despise your gifts, Lord.

" . . . One nation, divisible, with liberty and justice for some."

"They have mouths, but do not speak;
    They have ears, but do not hear; noses, but
do not smell."
        Tear the scales off of our eyes, Lord.
        Make us hear and smell.
        Enable us to speak the truth, Lord.

"Take away from me the noise of your songs; to the melody of your harps I will not listen.

But let justice roll down like waters, and righteousness like an ever-flowing stream."

Amen. Amen. Amen, Lord.

Tomb of the Unknown Soldiers and Civilians

Cloak and Dagger

Seal our bodies, minds and souls with honesty, Lord.

Keep us from big and small lies. Restrain us from subterfuge and every form of private or public deceit.

Enable us to be open to one another, trust each other, and live peacefully in a society where integrity and idealism are treated as if they were realities. Lord, let us make them realities.

Are we powerless to change realities that threaten our life, Lord?

I get mad when all the blame and the expense seem to be piled on top of me. Why doesn't somebody say what the individual can do to change the system?

Help us, Lord, not to commit suicide.

" . . . Power to the President . . . !"

"God spake these words and said: I am
the Lord thy God; Thou shalt have no other
gods but me."
 God, help us to obey your commandment.

127969

We pay for the hurts and wrongs that we inflict upon others, don't we, Lord?

There seems to be a law of compensation in life. If we do monstrous things against other people, we turn into monsters.

Turn us around, Lord.

Civilian Casualty in Indochina

We think that we're indispensable, or at least safe, and suddenly find out that we're not.

Whom can we trust, Jesus?

"Ollie, have you ever thought of doing a single?"

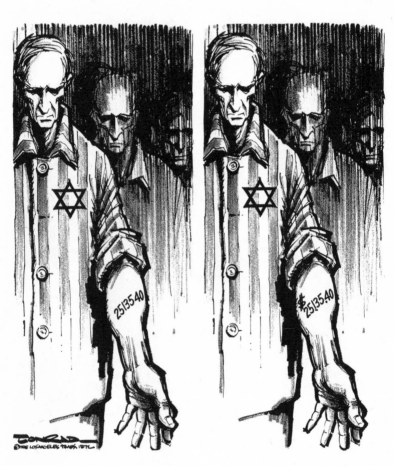

Germany - 1936   Russia - 1972

You want me to love these victims of the world's cruelty as I love myself, Lord.

How can I express my love in any concrete and helpful way? How can my love save lives, restore justice, and become a real force?

Christ, *move* my mind.

Christ, *move* my heart.

Christ, *move* my soul.

Christ, *move* my body.

Make me ready to make costly sacrifices, Lord, for your sake.

"**We do not** see our signs;
    there is no longer any prophet,
    and there is none among us who knows
how long."
    Too much innocent blood is on the hands
of false prophets, isn't it, Lord? Enable us to
see our signs, Christ.

We all use so many words, Lord, yet don't manage to communicate.

Let us say what we have to say, Christ, so that we may clearly understand one another.

"He says he's from the phone company . . ."

Somebody said, Christ, that we should avoid the appearance of evil as much as evil itself.

What can we do about our appearances of evil? I suppose, Lord, that the best thing is to throw as much light as we possibly can into dark corners.

Forgive us our trespasses, as we forgive those who trespass against us.

"You are typical American housewives . . . Do you think food prices are too high?"

"It is better to take refuge in the Lord than to put confidence in princes."

People who live in palaces should trade places every so often, it seems to me, Christ, with people who live in ordinary places.

I imagine that many of their opinions and attitudes would change pretty abruptly. Wouldn't it make for a saner world, Lord?

Life is funny as it is sad, Lord.

It would help, though, wouldn't it, if we could laugh at ourselves, as much as other people laugh at all of us?

The sap is running in the maple trees of New Hampshire

This is your FBI

It makes me feel sad when people's reputations are tarnished and sometimes destroyed, Lord.

Please give us strength to live up to our reputations.

He's a nut all right . . . But, maybe he's what the country needs . . . Somebody to really shake it up!''

Demagogues appeal to our fears, hates and insecurities, Christ, and make fools of us, don't they? They don't respect us or anybody else as persons.

Lord, don't let demagogues make victims of us.

Arrogance is dangerous, isn't it, Christ?

It can lead to isolation, pride that gets out of all control—and murder.

Isn't love the best alternative to arrogance, Lord?

Why do we play games with human lives, Lord?

If we got down to the nitty-gritty God business of practicing integrity in political ethics, and decency in treatment of the poor and dispossessed, we would serve you far better than looking pious in public, wouldn't we, Christ?

"O Lord, how manifold are thy works!
In wisdom hast thou made them all;
the earth is full of thy creatures."
You move in mysterious ways, Lord, to
perform your wonders.

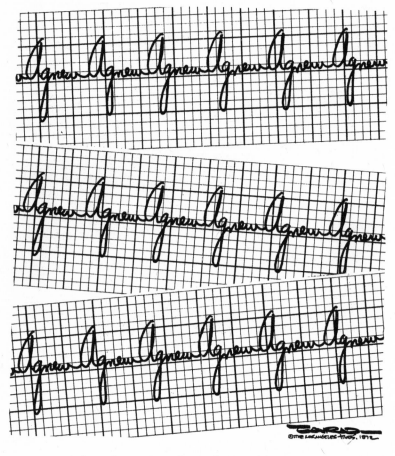

A heartbeat away from the presidency

Spiro Agnew spoke of "the glib, activist element who would tell us our values are lies." He proposed "to separate them from our society with no more regret than we should feel over discarding rotten apples from a barrel."

This seems to equate all dissent with treason, Jesus. Yet isn't principled dissent a form of prayer for America, Lord?

Some people pray to you, Lord, asking for strength and guidance in order to kill people, whom they call the enemy, and to destroy their land.

Can prayers be sins, Lord?

"Vietnamization is virtually complete."—Sec. of Defense Laird

"Era of Reconciliation"

Give us the vision and the guts to practice
what we preach, Lord.

When we become lunatics, please bring us back to our senses before we hurt anybody else too badly, Lord.

"Why not a simple constitutional amendment declaring
the courts unconstitutional?"

"Oh, it's just kind of a hobby with me . . . !"

Some people, Lord, seem to say "Thou shalt kill thy neighbor as thyself."

How can we have peace with guns in our hands, Christ?

Amen.

"I PRAY HEAVEN TO BESTOW THE BEST OF BLESSINGS ON THIS HOUSE AND ALL THAT HEREAFTER INHABIT IT. MAY NONE BUT HONEST AND WISE MEN EVER RULE UNDER THIS ROOF."

PRAYER BY PRES. JOHN ADAMS

Future Shock, Hell!

Once it was the future that frightened me, Lord. But sometimes now it is how will I get through this year, this month, or just today.

Please remind me again that I'm not a cipher, Christ. Let me know that I possess the worth of having been created in your image.

I am alive and a person, Lord, and I want to stand on my two feet and tackle problems with hope.

Shield us, Lord, from the temptations of evil.

Shield us, Lord, from the fruits of evil.

"But, first a word from our sponsor . . . "

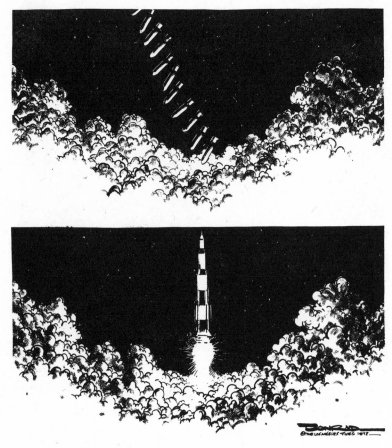

The Agony and the Ecstasy

It seems to me that there is a world of difference between hell and heaven, Jesus.

Save me from hell. Let me have a glimpse of heaven. But I'd rather have that glimpse of heaven right here on earth, Lord, instead of somewhere distant in faraway clouds.

When ideals go awry, and belief is transformed into cynicism, vivify our hearts and souls, Lord.

After we have slept, we need to be awakened.

"I'd like to see my lawyer . . . !"

"**I was hungry** and you gave me food. I was thirsty and you gave me drink. I was a stranger and you welcomed me. I was naked and you clothed me. I was sick and you visited me. I was in prison and you came to see me."

You told us, Jesus, that as we treat the least of your brethren in the world, so we treat you.

Please help us to treat you better, Lord.

Get into our consciousness, Lord, the idea that we can't save anything by destroying it.

"It became necessary to destroy the political electoral
system to save it."

"Someday, President Thieu, all this will be yours!"

Having some things is hell, isn't it, Jesus?

When our words are a mockery of decent truth and simple feeling, Christ, grant us the holy grace of respectful silence.

The tables can turn so quickly in life,
Lord. Will you teach us about the quality of
mercy?

"I know some good psychiatrists! . . . specialists on
depression!"

"We don't stop at schools anymore . . ."

"The Lord is my shepherd, I shall not want.''

What are we supposed to do, Christ, when our worldly shepherds fail us, lie to us, betray us, and even lead us unto evil?

Christ, what are we supposed to do?

I have always hoped, Lord, that the end of our human journey would be the center of light.

But are we going to find ourselves in a pit of man-made darkness?

The tunnel at the end of the light

"Had it not been for the international campaign waged throughout the world, particularly in the socialist countries and the Soviet Union, I am certain I would never have been released from prison!"

From becoming so engrossed in ourselves that we cannot see the predicament of others, deliver us, Lord.

Save us from moral blindness.

It's wrong to use scapegoats, isn't it, Christ, to avoid facing our own guilt and wrongdoing?

How can we condone violence and murder for our own causes and wars, and then moralistically condemn the same tactics when our opponents employ them?

"I suggest we handle this as the Americans would . . .
locate the lieutenant in charge and courtmartial him!"

Some songs are very warlike ones, aren't they, Lord?

I prefer songs about peace, love and beauty, Jesus.

"Make a joyful noise to the Lord, all the earth; break forth into joyous song and sing praises!"

The Committee to Reelect the President crossing the
Watergate

God, help us to puncture the vainglory and pomposity that can be found in all of us.

Give us more belly-laughs about the humanness that we share, the good and bad things that we do, and the idiocy in which we sometimes indulge ourselves.

Cruelty breeds on itself, doesn't it, Lord?
The torturer becomes callous as he increases the excesses of his cruelty, and finally establishes torture as a way of life for those whom he oppresses.

You suffered cruelty as the victim at our hands in your life among us as a man, Jesus.

"If you don't like it here, why don't you people go back
where you came from!"

"Then he said, 'Let me go, for the day is breaking.' But Jacob said, 'I will not let you go, unless you bless me.' "

Thank you, Lord, for your saints of struggle who give us the example of tenacity and deep purpose.

126

I understand that my brother and sister are legion, Lord.

Jesus, don't let me deny their rights as persons by labeling them.

"The handwriting on the wall in the old folks home."

"That Democratic Convention is giving Democracy a
bad name!"

We run into deep trouble when we play roles in life, don't we, Lord?

You want us to be ourselves and not actors in a charade. But we think all the world's a stage, and that stage is fair game for our fantasies.

Protect us, Lord, from our fantasies when they become gaudy and dangerous.

Who says you can't get to city hall from here?

On a clear day you can see all the way downtown from here, Jesus. But how clear must it be for those who run the city downtown to see out here?

Human life can't separate itself from the rest of life in the world, can it, Lord?

It seems that everything will either live or die together, Jesus.

Quality of air improving, lakes and streams dirtier.
—Council on Environmental Quality

War Story

"Hear and hear, but do not understand;
see and see, but do not perceive."
Will we understand and perceive, Lord,
before it is too late?

"The nerve of the North Vietnamese! . . . exploiting
POWs and their families for propaganda!"

It seems to me that these hats don't fit, Jesus. They appear to be part of stage costuming that is put on to fit the scene.

For those who play the game, pawns are expendable, aren't they, Lord?

Help us to see ourselves as others see us, Lord, and to understand why.

"I'm sorry. . . .I don't recognize
any of them!"

If war means "to kill," what single word means "to live"?
Can we find it, Lord?

"God Bless America."

I'm sure that you do bless America, Lord, just as much as you bless Cambodia, Brazil, the Vietnams, France and Nigeria.

But what have we done to the original Americans? Teach us, Christ, how to bless one another inside America.

Bury My Heart at Wounded Knee

When we resort to duplicity and lies, our troubles multiply instead of going away, don't they, Lord?

Stir us to tell the truth and accept it.

The President asked in his "Watergate
Message" for the nation's prayers.

What does that mean, Jesus?

Prayers comprise actions even more than
words, don't they? And all of us are co-
creators with you in the continuing act of
creation.

So it seems to me that constructive criticism and honest dissent, coming from our
consciences, may be the finest prayers that we
can offer for the President. Do you agree,
Lord?

The Silent Majority

"But, George, if you stay on the ticket, we won't be discussing issues . . . just your credibility!"

The truth hurts a lot sometimes, Christ. When it's about me, and I'd rather not look at it too closely, please help me to look it straight in the face.

Help us not to talk out of both sides of our mouths, Jesus.

"When we fail to make the criminal pay for his crime,
we encourage him to think that crime will pay . . ."

Another U.S. withdrawal

How can we withdraw from the human heart, Lord?

Why do we try to call your crucifixion 2,000 years old, Jesus?